BENDING

FIRST POETS SERIES 9

 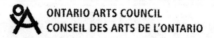

Canada Council   Conseil des Arts
for the Arts   du Canada

ONTARIO ARTS COUNCIL
CONSEIL DES ARTS DE L'ONTARIO

Guernica Editions Inc. acknowledges the support of
the Canada Council for the Arts and the Ontario Arts Council.
The Ontario Arts Council is an agency of the Government of Ontario.

DANE SWAN

BENDING THE CONTINUUM

GUERNICA

TORONTO·BUFFALO·LANCASTER (U.K.)

2011

Elana Wolff, editor
Guernica Editions Inc.
P.O. Box 117, Station P, Toronto (ON), Canada M5S 2S6
2250 Military Road, Tonawanda, N.Y. 14150-6000 U.S.A.

Distributors:
University of Toronto Press Distribution,
5201 Dufferin Street, Toronto (ON), Canada M3H 5T8
Gazelle Book Services, White Cross Mills, High Town, Lancaster LA1 4XS U.K.

First edition.
Printed in Canada.

Legal Deposit – First Quarter
Library of Congress Catalog Card Number: 2011921289
Library and Archives Canada Cataloguing in Publication
Swan, Dane
Bending the continuum / Dane Swan.
(First poet series ; 9)
Poems.
ISBN 978-1-55071-339-8
I. Title. II. Series: First poets series (Toronto, Ont.) ; 9
PS8637.W34B45 2011   C811'.6   C2010-907177-8

Contents

In loving memory of

Teacher Lewis,
Aunt Meggie,
& Rachel Martin

I

BETWEEN TWO WORLDS

The Irrelevant Age

In a world of hover-cars and space tourism
our last literary imprint
shall be   the emoticon –
elementary students
learning the difference
between colon open parentheses
and colon close parentheses.

Yeats, Shakespeare, Frost
still around
…works of this generation's authors
                    disposable.

Academics shall blame
Google Books® for our generation's demise
(the answer remains the same).

The answer remains the same
(k)no(w) matter how many times
you multiply zero.

The irrelevant age.

Lingo nonsensical.
Great works temporary.
Pivotal art lost on crashed hard drives,
degrading digital formats
as the floppy disk gives way
to the newest.

Generations later
the current technology
remains what it is
seconds after purchase:

an antique door stop.
Its treasures permanently locked
    within.

Pugilist

There's no place called paradise – just graces in time.

We shall melt
searching for fine grains of moments,

our heaviest punches
too light for us to be crowned.
Moments of our arms
raised before punch-drunk losses
have us returning to the gym.
       Sitting in the cut,
telling stories to future contenders,
remembering glimpses of nirvana.

These bloody knuckles are a drunkard's prize,
these empty bottles, a birthright.

In a dream, Nietzsche and Hegel
duke it out.

Fifteen rounds later
       time runs out.

Aerosol Acrylics

Lines that remember
this land before we knew time
are all that remain
of ancient
coniferous skyscrapers.

If all we are
is this existence
we are nothing more than
the marks left behind
by third-rate graffiti writers.

Hands covered with
acrylic renditions
of Pollock forgeries,
the outcome of scarred walls.
A pathetic avant-garde
(landscape remains).

Where wisdom once stood
concrete Neanderthals
adorn tomb sights:
inanimate misconceptions of beauty.

Needle/Vinyl

Dream at 33 1/3 revolutions per minute –
needle kisses vinyl, creating sweet music
          in worn grooves
as earth revolves around sun.

This is where dogs gain sophistication.
Where Afro-picks grow wild roots in fertile soil,
dispersing soul through canopies
– the tales this ancient record spins.

Watch her follow the grooves,
cracks and dirt – till she reaches
the turntable's axis;
unless, by chance, the record skips

the record skips

the record skips

Trying to Count Electric Sheep

Failed concrete poetry written in binary code
disguised as poorly constructed software
haunts my dreams.

Daymares of computer-error notices
while frozen web browsers
crash multiple personal computers simultaneously
        at 16:25 Greenwich Meridian.

Android pigeons sing lullabies to IT workers
as Apple© engineers laugh hysterically,
"I told you so," is not good enough.
Hexadecimals disintegrate.

Facing a blank screen – my data has faced mortality –
theories of the permanent inter-web
are chastised for their flaws.

We do not dream of electric sheep,
we count them in the prelude
as the new addition of DOS manipulating software
sings a laptop lullaby.

– You are not the only one who sees them –

The radiation bellows from their epidermis as
help-menus solve nothing,
and customer service recordings keep repeating,

Please press one for English

Harvey Philip Spector

For $20 you can block out the world, form a visual aesthetic from a stolen soundtrack. The score, composed of digital watermarks' uneducated ears, rarely perceived as mathematical pulses, puts oneself at ease. For $20-plus, a business woman can be made to sing burlesque standards in a mind's eye while skylarking hoodlums sing backup. For as little as $19.95, as much as $200, street vermin and shelter outcasts in the city core will sing rock ballads with the zeal of a Broadway chorus line. If you pay enough, clergy of various breadths of religion will proclaim the magic of sin through song and interpretative dance. For the right amount of legal tender every articulation will sound like a Tin Pan Alley enthusiast swindling you into believing they sing jazz. Grease the right palm and all the voices you hear in a day can be manipulated by tuning software or a vocoder. Your husband can sound like T-Pain; your wife Britney Spears. You've constructed a wall of sound between our worlds. As white cables ornate.

Ticket Counter

He asked us, "Why are you afraid of the white devil?"
Before I answered, three people lauded his racist
    rhetoric.

When it was my turn I simply said, "I and I fear no
    man."

We wear our neighbourhoods like armour,
our hurdles like the Himalayas,
the city line like an electric fence.

We fear everything.

We're afraid of the cops,
afraid of people we don't know,
terrified of our so-called allies.

Afraid to leave.

Afraid to get on a bus,
stick our thumbs out,
take our cars and drive somewhere we feel safe.

Afraid to go.

Go it alone,
go where we are more of a minority
but feel loved.

Afraid of love.

It took thirty years to find courage, to find love,
seventeen for lust,
still searching for home.

The labour for love is ridiculous.
Maybe it's the work we fear.
It's fear that has us land-locked.

Afraid to leave the fear behind,
purchase a ticket,

depart.

Blackface

Petty frauds
masquerading misery.
Watch them tap-dance –
dressed as hobos;
false smiles and shimmies
seek your pity, your money.

They are not *the real McCoy*.

Witness the genuine dance.
Watch how the soul propels –
a pulse that moves the congregation
like an ancient tsunami of legend.
You will fall down –
may never stand back up –
because this is our bedrock.

Our savage sophistication
flows through the earth
like the energy of a Juju man.
You are now observing
trance inducing moments –
the seizures are nothing to fear.

See us levitate while standing
on solid ground;
awe-struck like the first time
humanity heard Mahalia wail.
Follow us on the dirt path
to a shack at the crossroads.

Take a glimpse inside.

Experience our truth.

A culture constructed
by stolen people
who remember this dance
despite the whips and chains.
…this music
despite the lynchings.
…this art despite the prisons,
slave ships, ghettos,
miseducation.

The system designed to squash us
we thrive through –
do not mistake us for weak.
Like the pillars that bound Samson,
some things are destined to crumble.
We have mastered
the art of impossible –
some swore we were devils
we should have fallen ages ago.

You'll be disappointed
if you thought
we'd shuck and jive on cue –
this dance is not for your entertainment.

This is a celebration,
a hallelujah,
a thank you to our ancestors,
a kiss to our mother who has
blessed our toil filled journey.

You're more than welcome to
join us on this trail.

To-Do

buy coffee

replace coffee grinders
used to "bust" weed with coffee cups

erase illogical conflicts
with calm conversation

evaporate

fold away the slow torture

preserve the imperfections

allow the sunrise

bend the continuum

remember everything

re-materialise in a new paradigm

make a fresh pot of coffee

The Largest Market in the World

Packed with people –
cashier at every register,
attendant behind each counter.

Shoppers fill the aisles,
wait patiently to be served,
admire their purchases:

baskets filled
with newborns
of every ethnicity,

shopping carts
crammed with toddlers
from around the world.

Window displays of models posing –
live re-creations
of renaissance statues.

The ultimate in retail –
men, women, and transgenders
shelved to the hilt.

Virile women
fight over the last straight
Adonis in stock.

The longest line?
Returns. Purchased products
rarely meet expectations.

Brothers

1. Yallas River Jamaica

Three naked boys,
unafraid of shrinkage
bathe naked in the ice-cold river.
Sun burns down on the shivering three,
too busy with a bar of soap to notice.
In the shadow of Blue Mountain
where coffee beans grow
they wash in water
siphoned for crops –
crops to pleasure buyers miles away.

2. Mango Season

Mango season means dad's buying fresh fruit
from the stand across from Zebra Field
while we wait in the Hyundai Pony.

Homemade bibs of napkins
cover our chests.

Old newspapers laid across the stoop –
the way it's done in art class at school.

Outdoor conversations with
our neighbours Howard and Claudette,
enjoying the seasonal treat.

Brothers three in the tanning sun;
faces, chests, and elbows
sweet with fruit
and genuine smiles.

Queen of Hearts

"If you go back to Bermuda I'll leave you."
On another astral plane I took my cue –
took the bus to Pearson,
flew to a friend's embrace,
betrothed her, settling for middle class.

There was a miscue; I stayed.
We showed one another ugliness,
blamed everything but the mirror.

After our five-year winter
I fell for the Queen of Hearts.
She showed me Spring,
helped me clear a path,
taught me to not worship the past.

On the new moon she takes me
to see the other me:
I tuck my children in; double-date myself.

Dionaea muscipula

Her pheromone perfume
   magnetic.

All of us insects
destined to be meals,
our hearts mere refuse.

Beware the flower
who speaks of Venus.
She may have you for breakfast.

Reverse

I whisper secrets
to elderly moths,
pretending they're butterflies.

I hope they fly south,
gorge on milkweed,
become Monarchs.

I dream they reverse existence –
return to cocoon,
re-emerge to majesty.

II

A Dozen Red Roses

1

She asked for
a dozen red roses.

He buys her
twelve
pots,
soil,
fertilizer,
and seeds.

Promises
to
share
all watering responsibilities.

2

She asked.
He waited.

Rewarded with a dozen kisses,
his face rose red.

She represents his greatest dreams,
daymares that this is fleeting.

Love became her fiction at twelve

but this is something true –

a dream to share.
And if there's only enough for one,

give all.
For botany is more than

seed, sun, chlorophyll, and water.
The agriculturist has divine responsibilities.

3

Twelve terracotta pots –
born of earth, care and affection for craft.

Baked in a kiln
and shelved by minimum wage.

Bearing the burden of imperfect hands,
these pots adorn her doorway –

twelve, in rows of three; seed flags, ornaments,
a letter.

4

The earth is alive –
don't you believe me?
Earth without nutrients is sand
and even sand is animate.

Did you know the pink sands of Bermuda
are made of crushed seashells,
bits of coral reef,
and a red single-cell species called foram?

This soil does more than
provide nutrients for seeds.
This deep-brown breathes.

5

I will be called beautiful at my death
as in life I am a symbol of both
love and unrequited love.

6

Now what a diss.
De man dem give we
a whole heep a clay pots
and dirt, and seed and ting
and chat rey rey poetry to I 'n' I
bout waterin' responsibilities.
If me na love dat po' soul
me a knock off his block ya know,
but we love dat idiot bwoy,
dat fool a my fool ya know
serve we right fi
tell a stupid man to buy we roses.
Now me stuck water de blessed tings.

7

Do the bud and bloom
spell flourishing love?

What of the stem and thorn?

8

From the melting ice cap,
acidic precipitation,
contaminated stream,
diseased river
to filtration system.
From the filter
to the filter
add more chemicals.
From the waterway,
the bathroom tap,
the watering can,
the spray bottle.
To leaves,
to stem,
to soil
and roots.
Add sun,
lamp-heat,
and feed.

9

Have you seen the rose shrub,
gangly with spikes.
If lucky it flowers each year.

Be forewarned:
This plant tears the skin of those it snags.

10

Now and then, stop and smell them,
concentrate on the details.
Step into the world beyond your door.
Reality is more than stamen, ovum;
the most dynamic *Rosaceae*
comes from cross-pollination

Superior,
Inferior.
Like flowers, judged by our organs –
red means love; yellow
friendship.
Maybe it's time to be colour-blind.

11

Her sweat carries the essence of rose water.
Working fourteen hours a day for pennies handling
    roses
will do that.

Wearing the gloves her mother bought, she cuts and
    clips
in the cooler.
Daughter wants to be like mother.
They have very little money,
but the roses are beautiful.

He makes fruit punch with rose water.
It reminds him of the years he lived with his
    grandmother.
He grows roses on his windowsill.
His lover loves the flowers, and him.
He has very little money,
but the roses are beautiful.

She washes her floors with soap, water, and rose water.
It takes her back to the days when she'd chat with the
    maid –
the only person there when her husband died.
The maid, who was deported on a technicality, loved
    roses.
She had very little money.
But the flowers were beauties.

12

If twelve red roses express undying love,
do eleven represent love expiring?
Thirteen, a raptured passion?
Fourteen blood-reds, obsession?
Half a dozen, love beginning?

What about a dozen buds?
Or seeds
with half the labour pledged?

III

UNECLIPSED

Cuppa Tea

I's supposed to be a millionaire by forty
Means I should've had
FIVE HUNDRED THOUSAND by now
Should be wearin' a suit and tie by now

Be a big roller

I know an ol' businessman
He got tired and retired that world
He and I sip tea at his place –
'Round a table tales unfurl

Mine about such trivial struggles
His of wisdom in dis world
I'm so jealous he got money
He so jealous I got a girl

I don't think we'd ever change place –
these seats suit us fine.
I kinda like his company
I'm sure dat he likes mine.

Coffee Time

If the sign did not say
Patrons have a 20 minute time limit
we would not feel welcome.
(We should have higher standards.)

Maybe we can push our luck,
stay here for 40,
see if the retiree behind the counter
points to the sign, shows us
the door.

I remember when nefarious types
filled this place, now a few
seniors shoot the breeze –
about why they quit their crappy jobs.

4 coffees, 3 doughnuts, 1 beef patty.
Our table sits below the lone wall clock.
Making the most of our 20 minutes,
we slink into warm old conversations,

play three games of hangman
with misspelled words,
eat our food, drink our coffees, and go.

The old man doesn't seem to mind
we took our time.

Civilized Poverty

On these blocks
we go out for breakfast
and eat dinner at home.
In summer, welfare cases
and E.I. scammers
lounge on thousand-dollar couches
with antique-furniture store owners.
Refreshments camouflaged by brown paper bags.

On these blocks
bug spray is for bed bugs,
roaches have nicknames
and the good
landlords
take months
to not fix a thing.
There's no place like home
when home is a blues song.

On these blocks
the mentally ill
beg the underemployed
for legal tender –
as if illness has value to the poor.
If it did, these sidewalks would be gold,
for our sickness is terminal.

On these blocks
sex workers, addicts, artists, pimps and students
know one another
by their Christian names;
oblivious to each other's daily activities,
tell tales in diners
that only sell breakfast.

West Southwest

This hour is ours and they are trespassing.
We are the spiritually impaired,
late-night workers,
club-goers,
drug fiends,
lust seekers,
victims of failed love.

There they are –

the audacity of some people,
awake on our time.
Their skin dark as night sky,
their garments *blanche magnifique*,
a divine glow.
Their child appears to have
reached enlightenment in paternal arms.
The cab driver they hail
stops despite their race.
Our bloodshot eyes
admire this holy black family.
For on the hour of West Southwest
they embody beauty,
while the rest of us resemble
patrons of public transit.

Broken Patois

For personal happiness, avoid the Queen streetcar –
especially on weeknights.

You'll hear him. In broken patois
calling someone a sanitary napkin burning in hell.
He curses club-goers, homosexuals,
those returning from late-night shifts.
Dress funny and he labels you a Satan-worshipper.

Those of us who understand are horrified.

He reminds us why we work:
to save up, find a better situation.
Giving all us islanders a bad reputation.
The rest of us hooray in whispers
as he disappears to the abyss –
one stop before Roncesvalles.

Being Black

is having
a family tree that begins
in South Carolina,

knowing two of your
ancestors were lynched –
thinking that's normal.

Not knowing what "the old country" means.

Watching women cross the street
to avoid you,
purses clenched. Being trusted
less than a sex offender.

Being introduced five times
to someone, still
they pretend
not to know you.

Being black is police harassment,
not getting jobs. An outsider
in your "home" land.

It's climbing mountainous hurdles
like speed-bumps,
seeing the burden as blessing.

Parkdale Snowstorm

The two of us,
caught in a snowstorm,
dusty, dingy Parkdale bar:
A couple, a bar maid,
a TV from the last century.
Watching empty streetcars
and a toothless passerby.
Soup cans in one hand,
a box of crackers the other.

The light from the vacuum-tube
warms us
as the bar maid peers at
the residue of dollar-store coffee-mugs.
My lives mimic Shakespeare agonists:
Othello, Lear, Macbeth.

Yours was singular –
each lifetime a chapter in the same novel.
Fascinated, the aging maid
re-examines your hand.

The age lines read you'll live forever.

Decrescendo

At what point did the penthouse
replace a green canopy?

Frenetic pace usurp stillness?

Long drives defeat long walks?

Tranquillity hindered,
melancholic beauty
now a chaotic collage.

Nostalgic daymares of pianissimo.

Antiquities

Old enough to be grandfather clocks. Dangling from handles like antique ornaments, their bodies, like pendulums, swing, despite the straight path of the bus. Blank faces show 4:35. Worn arms respond with a warm grasp of a shoulder, refusing a seat for a brief reprieve. I'm reminded of him as the bell tolls.

William

You tried to tell us stories from a mischievous adolescence; we pretended to be ninjas, inspired by Ultraman, your cigarette plumes our smokescreen. You sat in your favourite chair, embers glowing from your green-glass ashtray. The dust bunnies at your place were older than I am now; I discovered this playing hide-and-seek with the other grandchildren, great-nieces and nephews; never touching a broom, terrified one would bite. Cleaning was a time to run away. From this window you witnessed your grandchildren picking wild cherries and loquats from the same trees as your children before us. After Grandma died, you did this a lot. Watching in solitaire. Thirty years of looking at the world continue after yours had atrophied. I'm sorry for not being a better grandson.

Bored

She fits the image of fabulous vagabond:
today her dollar-store accessories
match her red-white attire,
rose-coloured glasses
held together by transparent tape.

Usually she's attentive.
Today her mouth is ajar,
her eyelids closed,
the outline of her voice-box on display.

Her chest is at rest.
Passersby think she's expired.
But when two approach,
as if on cue,
she promptly breathes,
then snores.

Jack of Spades

One night my dreams spoke –
told me my teeth would leave.
Molars, bicuspids, and canines
raining to the floor.

Where I once feared to be locked in,
deadbolt and chain
now comfortably ensure my capture.
(My pillows lie at the foot of the bed.)

This apartment: an agreeable grave.
Tomorrow I'll reach out,
watch my digits
dissolve into the ether
as the earth shakes,

play dominoes with a dark prince.

Gravity

Let us dissolve.
Let our works disappear.
Let our art add nothing.

Let us be academic.
Give blessings only to peers.
Leave mortals in a cursed land.

Let us fall
and reach below.
Let us evanesce.

Day, Night Sky

We are more than the eclipse,
variety
our beauty.
We are not the same.
Different tastes,
visions
unify.

We are not meant
to fit in boxes.
Tearing the cardboard,
we refuse
the crevice offered,
spread our wings
to open spaces.

We kiss passionately in public –
see the high wire as opportunity.
Suspended in air,
we liquefy the glass above us
with our radiance,
invoking proverbs of wisdom;
    uneclipsed.

On the Edge

some smile –
grins that celebrate
destination, inches
representing life.
    Others cry.
Tears of loss, steps
from joining loved ones
on the other side.

The view is beautiful here,
but no one leaves the tour bus.
They just scream obscenities
from open windows.

Luxury an arduous trek –
so children tuck telescopes
beneath beds. With hope
of dreaming distant futures.

This is where god lives.
At the place where earth ends.